Dan Coates
with you in mind

8 Original Piano Solos for Today's Pianist

To my father, Bill –
with gratitude for a lifetime
of encouragement and love.

Project Manager: Carol Cuellar
Art Design: Olivia D. Novak

Dan Coates □□□□□□□□□□□□□□□□□□□□

As a student at the University of Miami, Dan Coates paid his tuition by playing the piano at south Florida nightclubs and restaurants. One evening in 1975, after Dan had worked his unique brand of magic on the ivories, a stranger from the music field walked up and told him that he should put his inspired piano arrangements down on paper so they could be published.

Dan took the stranger's advice—and the world of music has become much richer as a result. Since that chance encounter long ago, Dan has gone on to achieve international acclaim for his brilliant piano arrangements. His *Big Note, Easy Piano* and *Professional Touch* arrangements have inspired countless piano students and established themselves as classics against which all other works must be measured.

Enjoying an exclusive association with Warner Bros. Publications since 1982, Dan has demonstrated a unique gift for writing arrangements intended for students of every level, from beginner to advanced. Dan never fails to bring a fresh and original approach to his work. Pushing his own creative boundaries with each new manuscript, he writes material that is musically exciting and educationally sound.

From the very beginning of his musical life, Dan has always been eager to seek new challenges. As a five-year-old in Syracuse, New York, he used to sneak into the home of his neighbors to play their piano. Blessed with an amazing ear for music, Dan was able to imitate the melodies of songs he had heard on the radio. Finally, his neighbors convinced his parents to buy Dan his own piano. At that point, there was no stopping his musical development. Dan won a prestigious New York State competition for music composers at the age of 15. Then, after graduating from high school, he toured the world as an arranger and pianist with the group Up With People.

Later, Dan studied piano at the University of Miami with the legendary Ivan Davis, developing his natural abilities to stylize music on the keyboard. Continuing to perform professionally during and after his college years, Dan has played the piano on national television and at the 1984 Summer Olympics in Los Angeles. He has also accompanied recording artists as diverse as Dusty Springfield and Charlotte Rae.

During his long and prolific association with Warner Bros. Publications, Dan has written many award-winning books. He conducts piano workshops worldwide, demonstrating his famous arrangements with a special spark that never fails to inspire students and teachers alike.

Contents

ONCE UPON ANOTHER TIME

By DAN COATES

Once Upon Another Time - 4 - 1

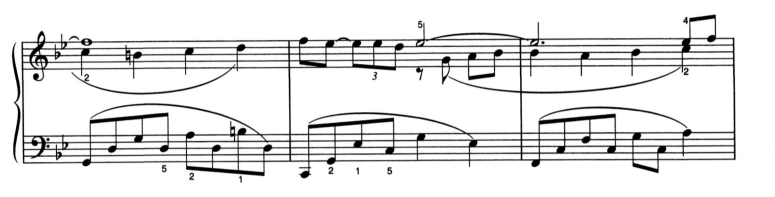

(2nd time, play R.H. one octave higher)

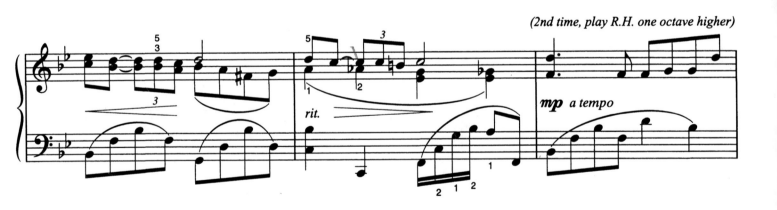

JAZZ IN 3

By DAN COATES

Bright jazz waltz ♩ = 156

Jazz in 3 - 5 - 1

Jazz in 3 - 5 - 2

Jazz in 3 - 5 - 4

Jazz in 3 - 5 - 5

CLASSICAL FOLLY

By DAN COATES

Allegro (♩.=142)

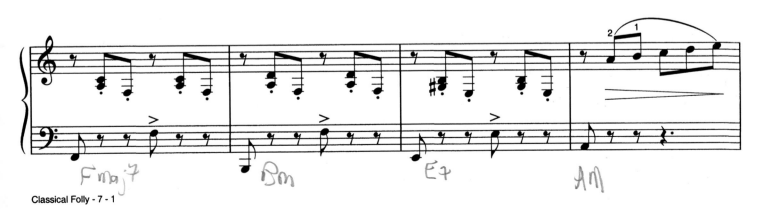

Classical Folly - 7 - 1

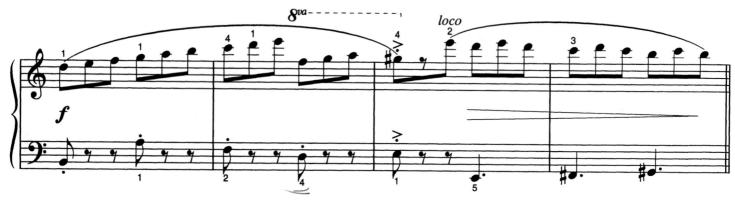

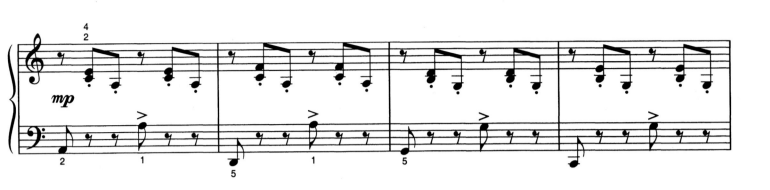

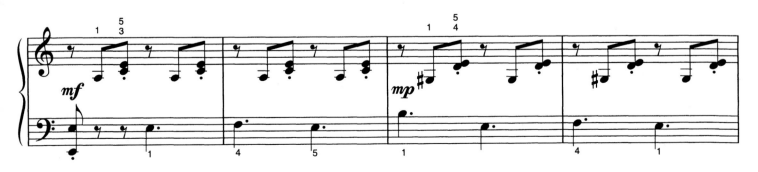

AUTUMN ETUDE

By DAN COATES

WIND-UP LULLABY

By DAN COATES

Slowly and tenderly

Wind-up Lullaby - 4 - 2

Wind-up Lullaby - 4 - 4

WITH YOU IN MIND

By DAN COATES

Slowly, with expression

With You in Mind - 4 - 1

CELEBRATION

By DAN COATES

With spirit (♩=112)

AT DAWN

By DAN COATES

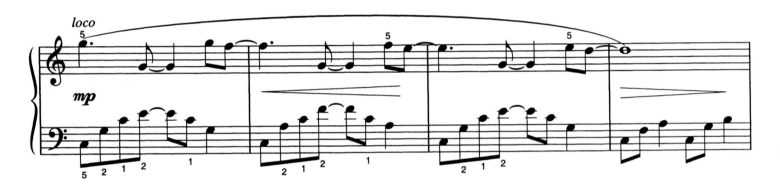

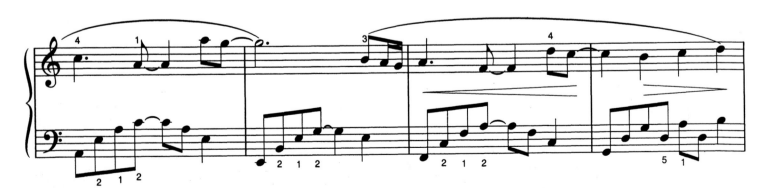

At Dawn - 5 - 1

At Dawn - 5 - 2

At Dawn - 5 - 4

Dan Coates...
The Best in Easy Piano

A Decade of Lite Hits: Contemporary Pop Ballads
(AFM00031)

A wonderful collection of some of the most beautiful pop ballads of the last decade expertly arranged by Dan Coates. Titles include: All My Life • Amazed • Angel Eyes • Back at One • Because of You • Candle in the Wind • Don't Cry for Me Argentina • From This Moment On • I Believe I Can Fly • I Do (Cherish You) • I Turn to You • In This Life • Love Will Keep Us Alive • The One • Sand & Water • Smooth • Sunny Came Home and many more.

The Hits of Elton John
(AFM01010)

Lush Dan Coates arrangements of 14 of Elton John's signature tunes including: Candle in the Wind • Daniel • Don't Let the Sun Go Down on Me • Little Jeannie • Nikita • The One • Sacrifice • Sad Songs (Say So Much) • Something About the Way You Look Tonight • Sorry Seems to Be the Hardest Word • Tiny Dancer • Your Song and more.

Pop Music Hits 2001
(AFM01016)

Twenty-five of the hottest pop hits by such artists as Lonestar, Faith Hill, Christina Aguilera, 98°, Jessica Simpson, Britney Spears, Backstreet Boys, Brian McKnight, ★NSYNC and more. Titles include: Amazed • Breathe • Come On Over (All I Want Is You) • Give Me Just One Night • I Think I'm in Love with You • I Turn to You • Lucky • My Everything • Shape of My Heart • Show Me the Meaning of Being Lonely • Stronger • That's the Way It Is • This I Promise You • Win and more.

Something More for the Boys
(AFM01007)

Music and songs from cartoons, movies, and television, as well as classic rock, modern rock, pop, and much more — titles that boys will really like! Titles include: American Pie • Change the World • Just Give Me One Night (Una Noche) • Hotel California • Lean on Me • (Meet) The Flintstones • "Jetsons" Main Theme • Olympic Fanfare and Theme • Smooth • Theme from *Inspector Gadget* and more!

Something More for the Girls
(AFM01008)

A fantastic collection of 21 songs that are favorites of today's pre-teen and teenage girls. They'll love the titles, which are straight from the top of the charts. Titles include: Graduation (Friends Forever) • I Hope You Dance • I Think I'm in Love with You • Lucky • Oops!...I Did It Again • Shape of My Heart • Stronger • That's the Way It Is • This I Promise You • A Whole New World and more!

AD1077 6/02

New Series by Dan Coates!

Teacher's Choice!
Dan Coates Pop Keyboard Library

Designed to work with any piano method, this series offers an outstanding source of pedagogically sound supplementary material that is fun and exciting and will appeal to today's piano student. Specifically graded and with fingerings at each level, these books will expand any student's course of study, giving them incentive to practice and play more.

- **The early levels (Books 1 and 2) have teacher accompaniment parts, and the titles have been carefully selected to appeal to the younger student (children's songs, patriotic music, folk songs, cartoon themes).**

- **Book 3 offers more pop titles, including music from *Harry Potter, Star Wars,* and even some Disney favorites.**

- **Books 4 and 5 (intermediate and advanced) cater to teen and adult players with great pop hits and standards, including the best movie themes and chart-topping pop ballads.**

BOOK 1, Early Elementary
Titles are: America, the Beautiful • Little Sir Echo • The Merry-Go-Round Broke Down • On Top of Old Smokey • Take Me Out to the Ball Game • This Land Is Your Land • This Old Man • Twinkle, Twinkle, Little Star • When the Saints Go Marching In • The Yankee Doodle Boy.
(AFM0205)

BOOK 2, Mid-Elementary
Titles are: Jeopardy Theme • Lullaby and Goodnight • The Muffin Man • Ode to Joy (Theme from Beethoven's *Ninth Symphony*) • Over the Rainbow (from *The Wizard of Oz*) • She'll Be Coming 'Round the Mountain • The Song That Doesn't End • This Is It! (Theme from "The Bugs Bunny Show") • Today • You Are My Sunshine.
(AFM0206)

BOOK 3, Late Elementary
Titles are: Daisy, Daisy • (Meet) The Flintstones • Happy Wanderer • Harry's Wondrous World (from *Harry Potter and the Sorcerer's Stone*) • I Believe I Can Fly • I've Been Working on the Railroad • Somewhere Out There (from *An American Tail*) • Star Wars (Main Title) • Theme from *Ice Castles* (Through the Eyes of Love) • Theme from *Inspector Gadget* • Tomorrow • A Whole New World.
(AFM0207)

BOOK 4, Early Intermediate to Intermediate
Titles are: Candle in the Wind • Circle of Life • Hedwig's Theme (from *Harry Potter and the Sorcerer's Stone*) • I Hope You Dance • In Dreams (from *The Lord of the Rings*) • The James Bond Theme • The Pink Panther • Send in the Clowns • Somewhere My Love (from *Dr. Zhivago*) • Theme from *E.T. (The Extra-Terrestrial)* • To Love You More • Your Song.
(AFM0208)

BOOK 5, Late Intermediate to Advanced
Titles are: All By Myself • Amazed • Don't Cry for Me, Argentina (from *Evita*) • From This Moment On • The Prayer • Somewhere in Time • Somewhere Out There • Theme from *Schindler's List* • Time to Say Goodbye • Valentine.
(AFM0209)

AD1099 1/03